WORST OF THE WORST

VOLCANIC ERUPTIONS!

by Aaron Sautter

CAPSTONE PRESS
a capstone imprint

Published by Capstone Press, an imprint of Capstone
1710 Roe Crest Drive, North Mankato, Minnesota 56003
capstonepub.com

Library of Congress Cataloging-in-Publication Data is available on the Library of Congress website.

ISBN: 9798875245053 (hardcover)
ISBN: 9798875245008 (paperback)
ISBN: 9798875245015 (ebook PDF)

Summary: Step into the fiery past and explore the world's deadliest volcanic eruptions—from the explosive 1980 Mount St. Helens' eruption to the catastrophic 1883 Krakatoa explosion and the infamous Mount Vesuvius disaster that buried Pompeii. Packed with real-life survival stories, breathtaking images, and must-know facts, this is your crash course into history's most extreme volcanic eruptions!

Editorial Credits
Editor: Donald Lemke; Designer: Tracy Davies; Media Researcher: Svetlana Zhurkin; Production Specialist: Whitney Schaefer

Image Credits:
Associated Press: New Zealand's Ministry of Foreign Affairs and Trade, 26; Bridgeman Images: © Look and Learn, 16, Photo © CCI, 8, Photo © North Wind Pictures, 17; Dreamstime: Enrico Della Pietra, 9; Getty Images: 500px/Petru Funar, cover, AFP/Matangi Tonga/Mary Lyn Fonua, 27, Bettmann, 19, Henri Leduc, 4, Hulton Archive, 15, j_renArt, 5; Newscom: akg-images, 7; Science Source: Claus Lunau, 11, Simon Terrey, 28; Shutterstock: Ahsanjayacorp (lava design element), cover (top) and throughout, It's ORA (volcano icon), spine and throughout, Valerii_M (mountains design element), cover (bottom) and throughout, VVadi4ka (torn paper), cover and throughout; USGS: 12, 13, 21, 23, J.G. Rosenbaum, 24, Lyn Topinka, 25, Pat Shanks, 29

Printed in the United States 6603

TABLE OF CONTENTS

Words in **BOLD** are in the glossary.

INTRODUCTION

EXPLODING MOUNTAINS

RUMBLE! The land shakes around a large mountain. *CRACK!* A large crack opens up in the ground. *KRAKA-DOOM!* Suddenly, the mountain blows its top!

Volcanic **eruptions** can be giant disasters. They can destroy towns and kill many people. Prepare to discover some of the worst volcanic disasters of all time.

CHAPTER 1

BURIED BY VESUVIUS

DISASTER STATS

Date: October 79 CE
Location: Mount Vesuvius, Italy
Lives Lost: about 16,000

It was a normal day for people living near Mount Vesuvius. But things changed quickly at about noon. First, the ground rumbled and shook. Then the mountain exploded! Huge clouds of smoke and ash were thrown miles into the sky.

Mount Vesuvius erupted near the ancient Roman city of Pompeii.

Throughout that day and night, hot **pumice** stones rained on nearby towns. The next day, huge **pyroclastic** flows of burning ash and mud buried the towns. People who hadn't escaped were killed instantly. It was the deadliest volcanic event in Italy's history.

Ash and mud surged into Pompeii, Italy.

A plaster cast of a victim of the Mount Vesuvius disaster

FACT!

Many open spaces were left in the ash by the bodies of the dead. In the 1860s, plaster casts were made of these spaces. The spooky casts show the positions the victims were in when they died.

CHAPTER 2

TAMBORA BLOCKS THE SUN

Date: April 1815
Location: Sumbawa Island, Indonesia
Lives Lost: at least 100,000

The deadliest volcano of all time exploded in 1815. Mount Tambora blasted so much ash into the **atmosphere** that it spread around Earth. This caused global cooling. Crops often failed for the next few years. This led to starvation and disease. Tambora is blamed for killing at least 100,000 people worldwide.

An illustration of the inside of Mount Tambora during its eruption

FACT!

North America and Europe saw snow and frost through the summer of 1816. It became known as the "Year Without a Summer."

CHAPTER 3

ALASKA'S BIG BANG

DISASTER STATS

Dates: June 6–8, 1912
Location: Alaskan Peninsula, United States
Lives Lost: 0

Houses buried in ash from Alaska's Novarupta volcano

Remnants of the disaster still cover the river valley near Novarupta.

The biggest volcanic event in North American history happened in June 1912. For more than two days, Alaska's Novarupta volcano shot giant clouds of ash into the sky. It filled a nearby river valley with pumice and hot **lava**. Luckily, local people had already fled the area. There were no **casualties**.

FACT!

The river valley later became known as the "Valley of Ten Thousand Smokes." In the 1960s, NASA sent astronauts there to train for moon landings.

CHAPTER 4

KRAKATOA CATASTROPHE

DISASTER STATS

Dates: August 26–27, 1883
Location: Rakata Island, Indonesia
Lives Lost: more than 36,000

Tragedy hit Indonesia again in 1883. When Krakatoa exploded, the entire mountain was destroyed. It's thought that the explosion was four times stronger than the world's most powerful atomic bomb. Shockwaves from the blast circled Earth at least three times!

The Krakatoa explosion caused several huge **tsunamis**. Waves more than 130 feet (40 meters) high wiped out villages on Sumatra and Java. More than 36,000 people were killed by the tidal waves. It was the second deadliest volcanic disaster ever.

Tsunamis caused by Krakatoa lifted ships onto land.

FACT!

The Krakatoa explosion was the loudest sound ever reported. It was heard at least 3,000 miles (4,828 kilometers) away at Rodrigues Island near Madagascar.

CHAPTER 5

EL CHICHÓN RETURNS

DISASTER STATS

Dates: March 28–April 4, 1982
Location: Chiapas, Mexico
Lives Lost: at least 1,900

People thought that El Chichón was **dormant**. But in 1982 it blew its top. Nine villages were destroyed. At least 1,900 people were killed. Many farmers lost their crops and livestock. The disaster caused many millions of dollars in damage.

FACT!

The Volcanic Explosivity Index (VEI) is used to measure the size of volcanic eruptions. The scale is rated from 0 to 8.

CHAPTER 6

PINATUBO WAKES UP

Dates: June 12–15, 1991
Location: Luzon, Philippines
Lives Lost: at least 840

Mount Pinatubo was asleep for hundreds of years. But in March 1991, it woke up. It started with waves of small earthquakes. Then in June, the mountain was rocked by huge explosions. The volcano shot millions of tons of hot ash and gas into the sky. It was the second largest eruption of the 1900s.

Ash from the Mount Pinatubo eruption fell onto nearby cars and homes.

FACT!

Typhoon Yunya hit the Philippines at the same time that Pinatubo erupted. The storm's heavy rains mixed with the volcanic ash. This caused roofs to collapse, killing hundreds of people.

CHAPTER 7

MOUNT ST. HELENS' FURY

DISASTER STATS

Date: May 18, 1980
Location: Washington State, United States
Lives Lost: 57

Mount St. Helens had long been quiet. But that was about to change. In March 1980, the mountain shook with many earthquakes and small eruptions. Then the north slope began to bulge 5 to 6 feet (1.5 to 1.8 m) per day. Scientists knew something big was coming.

A small eruption of Mount St. Helens in spring 1980

On May 18, a giant blast ripped through the mountain's side. A cloud of ash rose 15 miles (24 km) into the sky. The blast leveled millions of trees and killed countless wildlife. Fifty-seven people were also killed. It was the deadliest volcanic disaster in U.S. history.

Deep mudflows from the eruption left their mark on the mountain's forest.

FACT!

Glaciers and snow on the mountain melted instantly. This caused flash floods of boiling ash and mud called **lahars** that caused even more damage.

CHAPTER 8

OCEAN EXPLOSION

DISASTER STATS

Date: January 15, 2022
Location: Kingdom of Tonga, South Pacific Ocean
Lives Lost: 7

Hunga Tonga-Hunga Ha'apai was a tiny island. But it was really the top of a big underwater volcano. In January 2022, it exploded in one of the biggest eruptions ever.

Beach resorts destroyed by the Hunga Tonga-Hunga Ha'apai eruption

It blasted ash 36 miles (58 km) high. It also created large tsunamis that caused widespread destruction. Thankfully, few people were killed in this disaster.

FACT!

The Hunga Tonga event caused the biggest lightning storm ever recorded. Experts believe the ash cloud created more than 2,600 flashes of lighting per minute!

CHAPTER 9

A SLEEPY GIANT

DISASTER STATS

Date: unknown
Location: Wyoming, United States
Lives Lost: unknown

Did you know a **supervolcano** lies under Yellowstone National Park? This giant volcano last erupted about 640,000 years ago. If it erupts again, it could cause destruction across half of the United States.

Imperial Geyser hot spring pool in Yellowstone National Park

Thankfully, scientists are watching Yellowstone closely. There will be plenty of warning before this giant wakes up.

FACT!

Yellowstone is famous for its hot springs and **geysers**. These features are created by volcanic activity deep underground.

GLOSSARY

atmosphere (AT-muh-sfeer)—the whole mass of air surrounding the Earth

casualty (KAZH-uhl-tee)—injury or death from an accident

dormant (DOHR-muhnt)—not active but capable of becoming active

eruption (ih-RUP-shuhn)—the act of bursting forth or exploding with force

geyser (GY-zur)—a spring that now and then shoots out hot water and steam

lahar (LAH-har)—a moving fluid mass composed of volcanic debris and water

lava (LAH-vuh)—melted rock coming from a volcano

pumice (PUHM-iss)—a light glass formed by the rapid cooling of lava from volcanoes

pyroclastic (py-roh-KLA-stik)—rocks and rock fragments ejected from a volcano during an eruption

supervolcano (SOO-puhr-vahl-kay-noh)—a larger volcano that can have massive eruptions, much bigger than regular volcanoes

tsunami (soo-NAH-mee)—a great sea wave produced especially by an earthquake or volcanic eruption under the sea

READ MORE

Murray, Julie. *Volcanic Eruptions*. Minneapolis: Abdo Zoom, 2025.

Owings, Lisa. *Volcanic Lightning*. Minneapolis: Bellwether Media, Inc., 2025.

Schaefer, Lola. *Dangerous Volcanoes*. Minneapolis: Lerner Publications, 2022.

INTERNET SITES

Active Wild: Famous Volcanoes
activewild.com/famous-volcanoes

Kiddle: Volcano Facts for Kids
kids.kiddle.co/Volcano

National Geographic Kids: 17 Explosive Volcano Facts!
natgeokids.com/uk/discover/geography/physical-geography/volcano-facts

INDEX

ABOUT THE AUTHOR

Aaron Sautter is an author and editor of dozens of cool books for young readers. He enjoys a wide range of subjects from dramatic history and sports to spooky aliens and fantastic creatures. Aaron lives in Minnesota with his wife and two children. In his spare time, Aaron enjoys cheering for the Minnesota Vikings and going for long walks with his goofy, lovable dogs.